A BOY NAMED MARY JANE

A BOY NAMED

MARY JANE

AND OTHER SILLY VERSE

BY WILLIAM COLE

ILLUSTRATED BY
GEORGE MacCLAIN

FRANKLIN WATTS | NEW YORK | LONDON | 1977

The following poems in this book have been previously published, in whole or in part, and we are grateful for permission to reprint them:

"A Boy Named Mary Jane," from *Cricket* Magazine, January 1974, copyright © 1974 by William Cole; "The Yes-Sir Grocer" (in part), from *Cricket* Magazine, December 1974, copyright © 1974 by William Cole; "After the Elephant Sneezed" (in part), from *Cricket* Magazine, January 1975, copyright © 1975 by William Cole; "Banananananananana," "How Sad," "News Story," and "A Love Story," from *Cricket* Magazine, July 1975, copyright © 1975 by William Cole. Macmillan London and Basingstoke: "A Song of Thanks," from *Allsorts 4*, 1971, copyright © 1971 by Macmillan London, Inc. Simon & Schuster, Inc.: "Just for a Change," from *The Second Poetry Drawing Book*, copyright © 1962 by William Cole and Julia Colmore. The Viking Press, Inc.: "Back Yard, July Night," from *A Book of Nature Poems*, copyright © 1969 by William Cole; "Dumbbell" and "Some Sights Sometimes Seen and Seldom Seen," from *Oh, How Silly!*, copyright © 1970 by William Cole; "Sneaky Bill" and "What a Beautiful Word!" from *Oh, That's Ridiculous*, copyright © 1972 by William Cole. World Publishing Co.: "Two Sad," from *A Case of the Giggles*, copyright © 1967 by William Cole.

Library of Congress Cataloging in Publication Data

Cole, William, 1919-
    A boy named Mary Jane, and other silly verse.
    SUMMARY: Twenty-four humorous poems include "Piggy," "Sneaky Bill," "After the Elephant Sneezed," and "Lies, All Lies."
    1. Nonsense-verses. [1. Nonsense verses. 2. Humorous poetry] I. MacClain, George. II. Title.
PZ8.3.C675Bq   811'.5'4   75–34091
ISBN 0-531-01144-5 lib. bdg.
ISBN 0-531-00394-9
Text copyright © 1977 by William Cole
Illustrations copyright © 1977 by Franklin Watts, Inc.

37,911

CONTENTS

ABOUT
THE AUTHOR

William Cole is the editor
of forty anthologies, most
of them collections of lit-
erature for children. His
own poems have appeared in
*Cricket, The New Yorker, At-
lantic,* and *Saturday Review.*
He is the author of "Trade
Winds," a column appearing
in *Saturday Review.*

A BOY NAMED
MARY JANE

SOME SIGHTS
SOMETIMES SEEN
AND SELDOM SEEN

You don't have to go very far
To see a boat towed by a car;
But to see a car towed by a boat
Is *really* a matter of note.

To see a truck pulling a horse
In a van is a matter of course;
But to see a horse pulling a truck
In a van is *extremely* good luck.

SNORKELING

This strange and wavering shape I see —
Is it a friend or anemone?

TWO SAD

It's such a shock, I almost screech,
   When I find a worm inside my peach!
But then, what *really* makes me blue
   Is to find a worm who's bit in two!

BANANANANANANANANA

I thought I'd win the spelling bee
    And get right to the top,
But I started to spell "banana,"
    And I didn't know when to stop.

CAN'T DENY IT

Tall people sleep more than short people,
    it's said,
And the reason is that they're longer in bed.

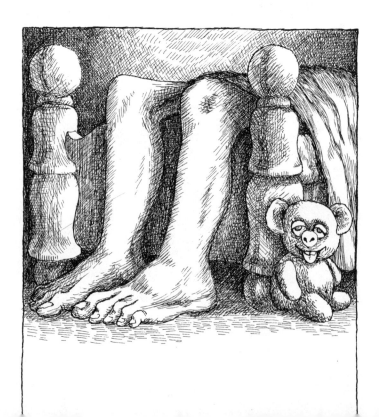

GOOD NEWS

The Board of Education has just set up new rules
That in the future they'll shut all the schools
On every April Fool's.

APRIL FOOL!
(Keep cool.)

NO

No birds, no flowers,
No sunshiny hours,
No days without rain
Or frost on the pane;
No fresh fruit is sold,
No weather but cold —
Please, Nature, remember:
Next year, skip November!

HOW SAD

There's a pitiful story — ah, me!
  Of a young English girl named Nellie,
Who stared dumbly all day at TV
  (Which in England is known as "the telly") —
She died . . . and the reason, you see,
  Was her brains had all turned into jelly!

NEWS STORY

When Peter Lumpkin was a youth,
    Imagine this! He lost a *tooth!*
When interviewed by a reporter
    He said, "You know, I found a quarter
Beneath my pillow — without doubt
    I ought to knock the *others* out.
I know I may look kind of funny,
    But goodness! I'll get lots of money!"

A LOVE STORY

"What are you doing now, my pretty maid?"
"I'm going to sneeze, kind sir," she said.
"You ain't gonna sneeze at me, are you?"
"Yes, I'm going to sneeze," she said, "AT–CHEW!"

PIGGY

For breakfast I had ice cream
   With pickles sliced up in it;
For lunch, some greasy pork chops
   Gobbled in a minute;
Dinner? Clams and orange pop,
   And liverwurst, sliced thick —
And now, oops! Oh, pardon me!
   I'm going to be sick!

DID YOU?

Having little kids around, they say, is truly bliss;
But did you ever hear of any little kid like this?

He swallows pits,
Has temper fits,
Spills the ink,
And clogs the sink.
And, oh my gosh!
He hates to wash!
He plays with matches,
And grabs and snatches.
He scrawls on walls,
And sprawls and bawls,
And argues and fights,
And kicks and bites. . . .
You say you never heard of
  any kid like that, you do —
Well, I know one who's
  just like that and it's
                        Y
                          O
                            U!

LIES, ALL LIES

There is no ham in hamburger,
    And "allspice" is a cheat;
Applesauce is not a sauce,
    And sweetbreads aren't sweet.

There is no horse in horseradish —
    Why are we so misled?
There's no cheese in a headcheese,
    And sweetbreads aren't bread!

LIARS' EXCHANGE

The first conductor yelled as loud
    As you'd shout "Fire!" —
    "EUreLIA! EUreLIA!"
The conductor in the second car
Shouted back, "EuRElia, EuRElia!"

WHAT A BEAUTIFUL WORD!

Ah, swallow . . . ah, swallow . . .
what a *beautiful* word!
(No, no! Not the gulp! I mean the *bird*!)

JUST FOR
A CHANGE

I wish that things didn't all have to be
The colors you always *expect* to see:

Just imagine a sky of green,
A sky that's never, ever seen;
And from it shines on everyone
A great big cheerful purple sun!

Over the grass of bright, bright red
Orange flowers and black are spread;
One other thing not seen before —
A silver house, a golden door. . . .

I know it sounds silly, crazy, and strange,
But *I'd* like to see it just for a change.

BACK YARD,
JULY NIGHT

Firefly, airplane, satellite, star —
How I wonder which you are.

FAT FELLOW

A man who weighed 'bout half a ton
  Went to the beach, and oh! what fun!

He plunged into the sea, and my!
The tide it changed from low to high!

DUMBBELL

My teacher is mad; he wants to know,
But I *can't* remember the Alamo!

THE YES-SIR GROCER

There was a grocer in our town
   who really was a pest,
He bragged that he had everything,
   and nothing but the best;
He huffed, "My store has got the
   greatest stock in all the land,
If I haven't got it fresh or froze,
   I've surely got it canned,
For I'm the 'Yes-Sir Grocer,'
   you just ask me and you'll see,
Nobody, but *nobody* has such a grocery!"

One day I thought, by golly,
   he should give his voice a rest,
I'll make a little list for him
   to put him to the test,
So I made up a list, I did,
   the list you see below,
And handed it to him that night
   when business seemed quite slow.
   IT READ —

   One bunch of melons, one ear of clams,
   One leg of prunes, a hand of hams;
   A cube of corn, a sheaf of tomatoes,
   An ear of lettuce, a jug of potatoes;

A clove of turnip, a chunk of beans,
A tube of bananas, two yards of sardines;
A sprig of eels, a bushel of cheese,
A grain of herring, a head of peas;
A stalk of butter, a bottle of beef,
A slice of rice, an asparagus leaf;
A piece of soup, a brussels sprout,
And half a bar of sauerkraut.

He read the list two times or three
   and turned as pale as death,
And said a few selected curses
   underneath his breath,
And then he looked back up at me
   with a kind of sickly smile,
And said, "You know, now, sonny,
   this will take a little while.

Just tell me where you want it sent."
   I answered with a leer,
"Thank you, Yes-Sir Grocer,
   but I'd rather eat it here."

I guess that was the final thing
   that sent him off his beam,
For he fell upon the counter with
   a kind of gurgling scream,
And he sobbed and bawled and
   hollered in a way to horrify;
It really was a terrible thing
   to see a grown man cry!
So I said, "I'm not a meanie;
   I was playing you a trick;
I know you've got a lovely store,
   but you lay it on too thick!"
And he answered, sobbing gently,
   that he guessed that I was right,
And I never heard him brag again
   since the "Yes-Sir Grocer" Night!

Did somebody say this is all untrue?
Now why in the world would I fib to you?
I've told the truth; I've done my best,
As sure as the sun rises up in the west.

A BOY NAMED MARY JANE

Once there was a little boy —
His name was Mary Jane —
Who lived 'way down in a tiny town
Called Washington, in Spain;
Whenever he went walking
He took his dog and cat;
His kitty's name was "Rover";
He called his doggie "Scat"!
     Is there anything wrong with that?

His mother was a plumber
With a heavy bag of tools;
His father taught crocheting
In all the local schools;
His sister was a boxer
(Her given name was Paul).
But Mary Jane himself had not
One single job at all
     (Because he was too small).

The summer he was two years old,
Or maybe in his teens,
His father went to Iceland
To buy some tangerines;
His mother went to Scotland
To play some basketball;

But Mary Jane he stayed at home —
He *still* was much too small —
    Till they returned next fall.

One day he said to Poppa,
"I don't know who's to blame,
But Holy Moses! Goodness' sake!
I do not like my *name!*"
His poppa said, "Now, Janey,
If two noble deeds you'll do
We'll think about another name
More suitable to you —
    Like maybe 'Kalamazoo'?"

So Jane went to the forest
And came upon a fish
Who'd tripped upon some seaweed.
(He heard it mutter, "Pish!")
It had a swollen ankle;
Jane fixed it with some string;

The fish hopped happily away
Waving with his wing.
    A most peculiar thing!

Then next week, in the ocean,
He came upon a cat
Who'd been out pleasure-swimming
And got bitten by a bat.
Jane soothed the wound with butter
(You'll find lots undersea)
And pussy was quite grateful:
"What noble deedery!"
    And Jane said, "Huh? Who *me*?"

And so he ran to Poppa,
And said, "Hey, listen, Dad —
Two noble deeds I've gone and did."
His poppa said, "Good lad —
I always knew you had the stuff;
Come shake my horny mitt;
I'll change your name to 'Oshkosh,' "
And Jane said, "Gosh! That's it!
    A really perfect fit!"

They all were very happy;
And I've got this to say:
Boys! If *you'd* be happy
You *must* learn to crochet!
And girls — you take up plumbing;
It's work that leads to fame;
And if you chance to have a son,
Don't cause him any shame —
    Let Oshkosh be his name!

SNEAKY BILL

I'm Sneaky Bill, I'm terrible mean and vicious,
I steal all the cashews
   from the mixed-nuts dishes;
I eat all the icing but I won't touch the cake,
And what you won't give me,
   I'll go ahead and take.

I gobble up the cherries from everyone's drinks,
And whenever there are sausages
    I grab a dozen links;
I take both drumsticks if
    there's turkey or chicken,
And the biggest strawberries
    are what I'm pickin';

I make sure I get the finest chop on the plate,
And I'll eat the portions of anyone who's late!

I'm always on the spot before the dinner bell —
I guess I'm pretty awful,
                              but
                               I
                                    do
                                      eat
                                         well!

A SONG OF THANKS

It's sensible that icicles
    Hang downward as they grow,
For I would hate to step on one
    That's buried in the snow.

It's really best that tides come in
    And then return to sea;
For if they kept on coming in
    How wet we all would be!

I've often thought tomatoes are
    Much better red than blue;
A blue tomato is a food
    I'd certainly eschew.

It's best of all that everyone's
    So tolerant today
That I can write this kind of stuff
    And not get put away.

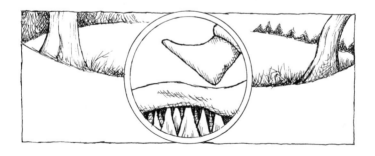

AFTER THE
ELEPHANT SNEEZED

I went to the animal fair,
The birds and the beasts were there,
The big baboon
By the light o' the moon
Was combing his auburn hair.

The monkey he got drunk,
He sat on the elephant's trunk;

The elephant sneezed,
And fell on his knees,
And that was the end of the monk . . .

But a voice was heard groaning "UNGK —
Get me out from under this lunk!
There's a chance I can squeeze
Out between these fat knees . . ."
It *wasn't* the end of the monk!

The juggler, a big polar bear,
Was tossing six balls in the air,
While he danced on his toes
And on top of his nose
He balanced a table and chair!

The lion said, "There's so much *space*
Whenever I walk anyplace —
I sure never would say,
'Hey! Get out o' my way!' "
But everyone did — just in case.

The sloth did some magical tricks,
Each one took five hours or six;
While doing each number,
He'd fall into a slumber,
But woke up when prodded with sticks.

The giraffe enjoyed being high;
The Ferris wheel reached to his eye;
So he placed himself there,
And throughout the whole fair
He talked to his friends riding by.

The baby aoudad he was bad,
And his aoudad daddy got mad
And tapped him a clout
On the side of his snout,
"Ow, Dad!" yelled the baby aoudad!

The cow muttered, "I'm such a prune;
I'm such an untalented goon —
I really feel thick —
I haven't one trick . . .
I guess I'll jump over the moon."

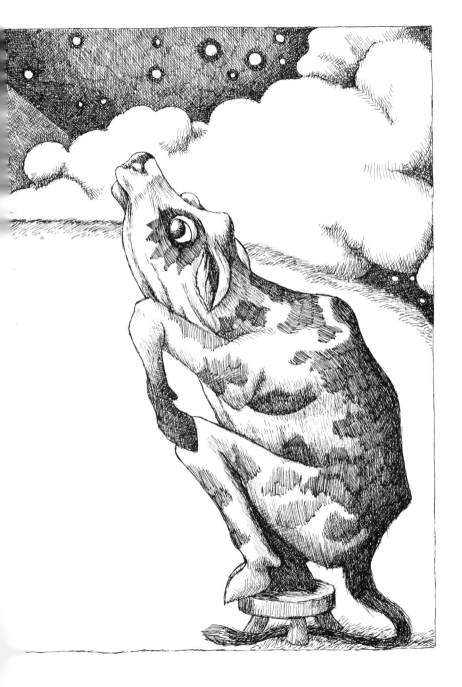

Then there were the lively young rats,
Who all were such great acrobats!
They said, "Oh, you'd learn
To twist, leap, and turn,
If you had to dodge from the cats!"

The chimp, with the greatest of ease,
Did tricks on the highest trapeze,
But he fell with a thump,
And got a small bump,
When he let go to scratch at his fleas.

The armadillo, named Andy,
Sold lighter-than-air cotton candy;
"If no one will buy,
It will float to the sky!"
And the crow said, "Oh, that would be dandy!"

The hippopot lady, named Ida,
Complained to Ramona, the spider,

"That horse won't agree,
But *I* want to be
Lovely Ida, the bareback rider!"

The peacock, an awful vain bird,
Croaked, "My, but I'm lovely! My *word!*"
"That's true," growed the gnu,
But your *voice* — ooh! ooh! *ooh!*
You're far better seen and not heard!"

The snake said, "I won me a *prize*"
(And tears trickled down from his eyes)
"I won me some shoes —
Which they *know* I can't use —
What's more, they're not even my size!"

Sue skunk was alone all the day —
Her booth was a perfume display.
"I just don't know why
  Nobody will buy —
They won't even *sample* a spray!"

Then the kangaroo hollered, "Ouch!
I just put me pipe in me pouch —
I sometimes forgit
The durn thing is lit!"
And shuffled away in a crouch.

Said the tiger, "It's one of my gripes
That I'm getting quite tired of stripes.
I'd like to arrange
To have spots for a change,
And be one of those leopardy types!"

The fox, always crafty and sly,
Shouted, "Hey, Look up at the sky!
It's *amazing*! Look! Look!"
Which they did, and the crook
Gobbled most of their ice cream and pie!

At midnight the well-combed baboon,
Announced by the light of the moon:
"I'm sorry to state
The hour is late —
We'd better be getting home soon."

The birds and the beasts who were there
All tossed their hats high in the air,
They all shouted, "Hooray!
What a wonderful day
We've had at the animal fair!"